GRAPHIC LIBRARY™

DISASTERS IN HISTORY

The TRIANGLE SHIRTWAIST FACTORY FIRE

by Jessica Gunderson

illustrated by Phil Miller
and Charles Barnett III

Consultant:
Clete Daniel, Professor of American Labor History
School of Industrial and Labor Relations
Cornell University, Ithaca, New York

Capstone
press

Mankato, Minnesota

Graphic Library is published by Capstone Press,
1710 Roe Crest Drive, North Mankato, Minnesota 56003.
www.capstonepub.com

Books published by Capstone Press are manufactured with paper
containing at least 10 percent post-consumer waste.

Library of Congress Cataloging-in-Publication Data
Gunderson, Jessica Sarah, 1976–
   The Triangle Shirtwaist factory fire / by Jessica Gunderson ; illustrated by Phil Miller and
Charles Barnett III.
       p. cm.—(Graphic library. Disasters in history)
       Includes bibliographical references and index.
       ISBN-13: 978-0-7368-5483-2 (hardcover)
       ISBN-10: 0-7368-5483-5 (hardcover)
       ISBN-13: 978-0-7368-6878-5 (softcover pbk.)
       ISBN-10: 0-7368-6878-X (softcover pbk.)
       1. Triangle Shirtwaist Company—Fire, 1911—Juvenile literature. 2. Clothing factories—
New York (State)—New York—Safety measures—History—20th century—Juvenile literature.
3. Labor laws and legislation—New York (State)—New York—History—20th century—Juvenile
literature. 4. New York (N.Y.)—History—1898–1951—Juvenile literature. I. Miller, Phil, ill. II.
Barnett, Charles, III, ill. III. Title. IV. Series.
F128.5.G95 2006
974.7′1041—dc22   2005029858

Art Direction and Design
Bob Lentz

Production Designer
Alison Thiele

Colorist
Buzz Setzer

Editor
Donald Lemke

Editor's note: Direct quotations from primary sources are indicated by a yellow background.

Direct quotations appear on the following pages:
Page 7, from Clara Lemlich's speech at Cooper Union, November 22, 1909, as quoted in
       Dave Von Drehle's *Triangle: The Fire that Changed America* (New York: Atlantic Monthly
       Press, 2003).
Page 8, from a speech on November 24, 1909, by Clara Lemlich, as quoted in Dave Von
       Drehle's *Triangle: The Fire that Changed America* (New York: Atlantic Monthly Press,
       2003).
Page 21, from an article originally published in the *Call,* November 23, 1909, as transcribed
       on Cornell University School of Industrial and Labor Relations' Kheel Center website
       (http://www.ilr.cornell.edu/trianglefire/texts/stein_ootss/ootss_sg.html).

Printed in the United States of America in Stevens Point, Wisconsin.
072012   006856R

TABLE OF CONTENTS

Chapter 1 STRIKE!

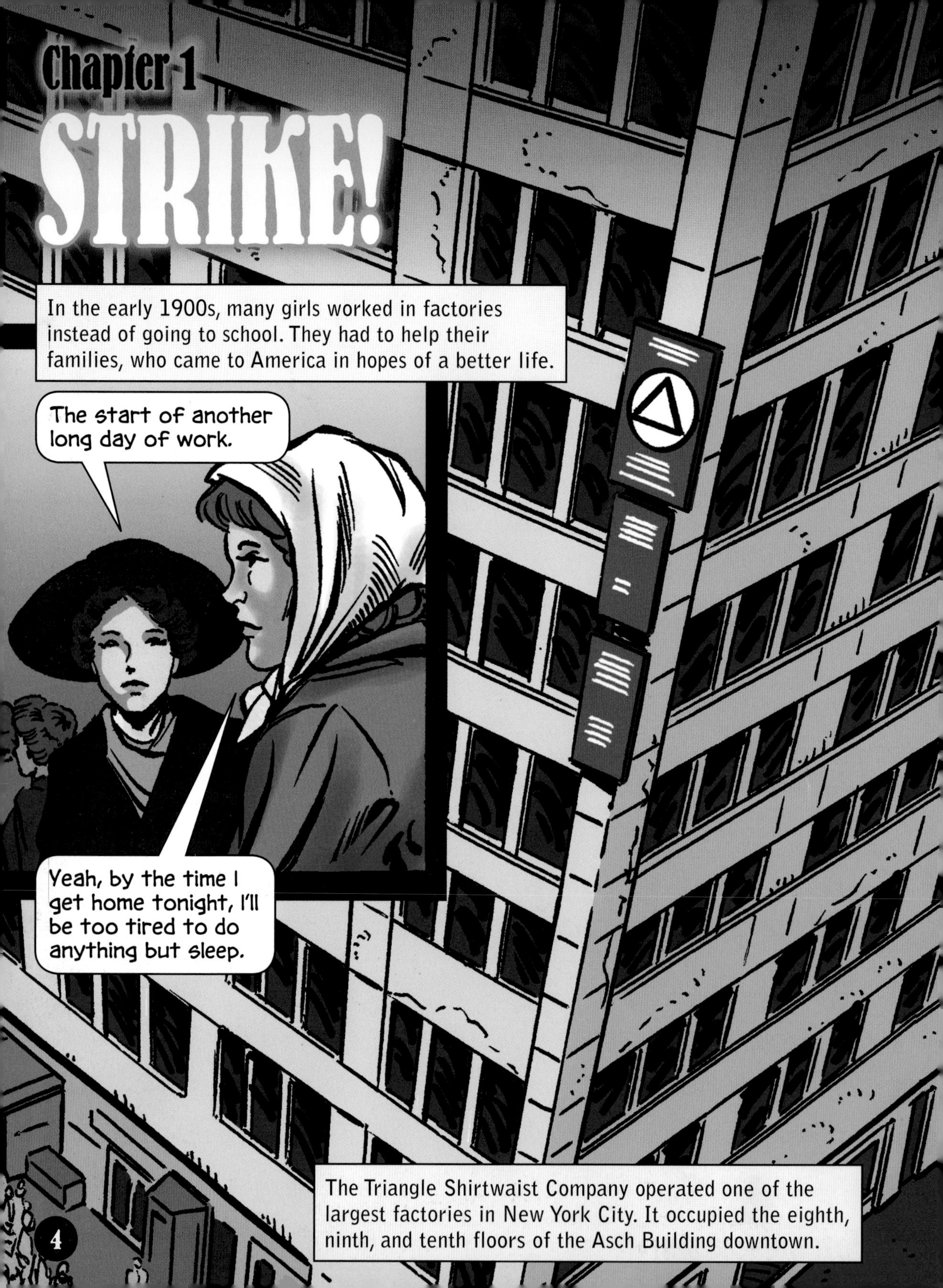
In the early 1900s, many girls worked in factories instead of going to school. They had to help their families, who came to America in hopes of a better life.
The start of another long day of work.
Yeah, by the time I get home tonight, I'll be too tired to do anything but sleep.
The Triangle Shirtwaist Company operated one of the largest factories in New York City. It occupied the eighth, ninth, and tenth floors of the Asch Building downtown.

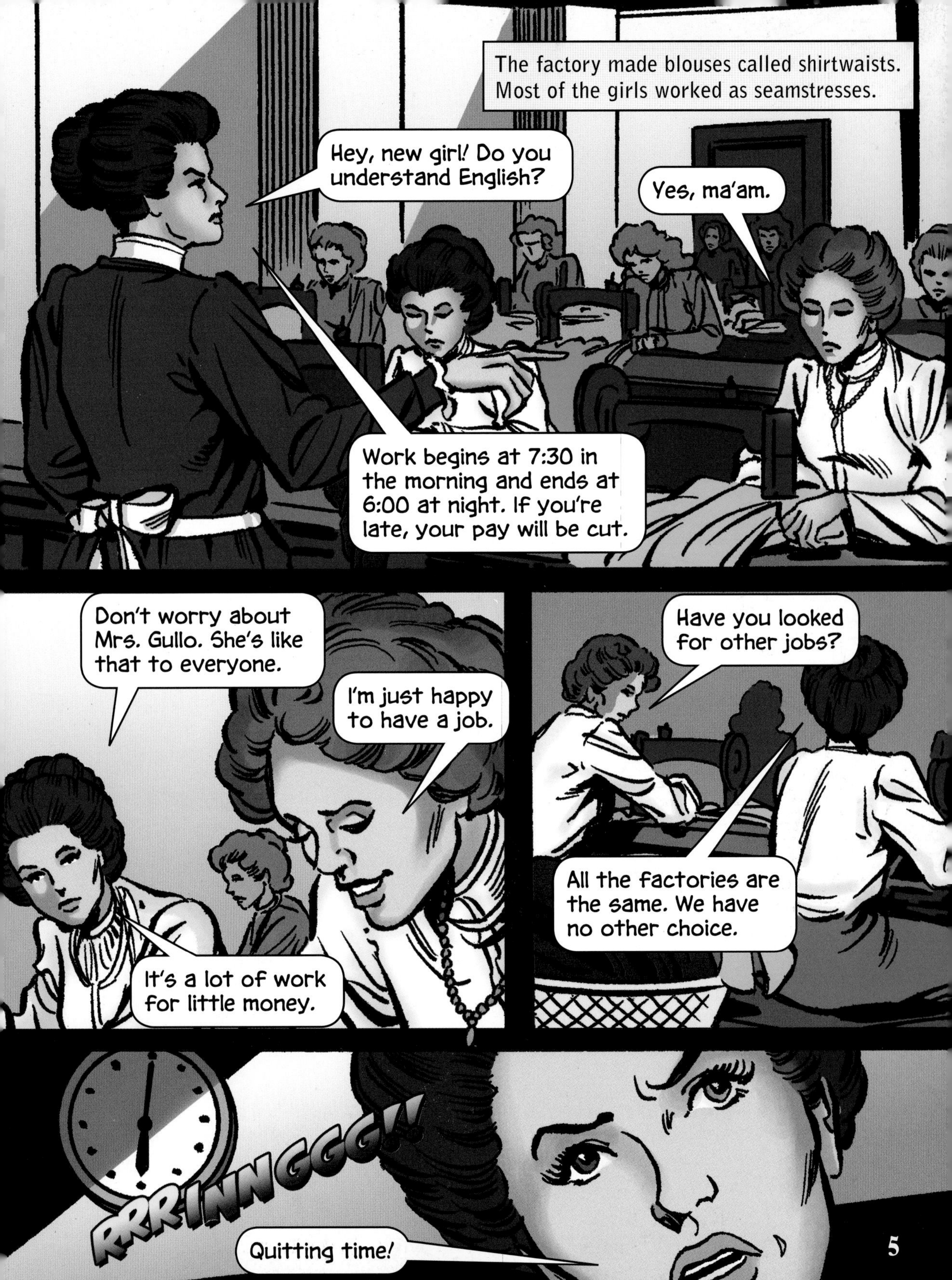
The factory made blouses called shirtwaists. Most of the girls worked as seamstresses.
Hey, new girl! Do you understand English?
Yes, ma'am.
Work begins at 7:30 in the morning and ends at 6:00 at night. If you're late, your pay will be cut.
Don't worry about Mrs. Gullo. She's like that to everyone.
I'm just happy to have a job.
It's a lot of work for little money.
Have you looked for other jobs?
All the factories are the same. We have no other choice.
RRRINNGGG!!
Quitting time!

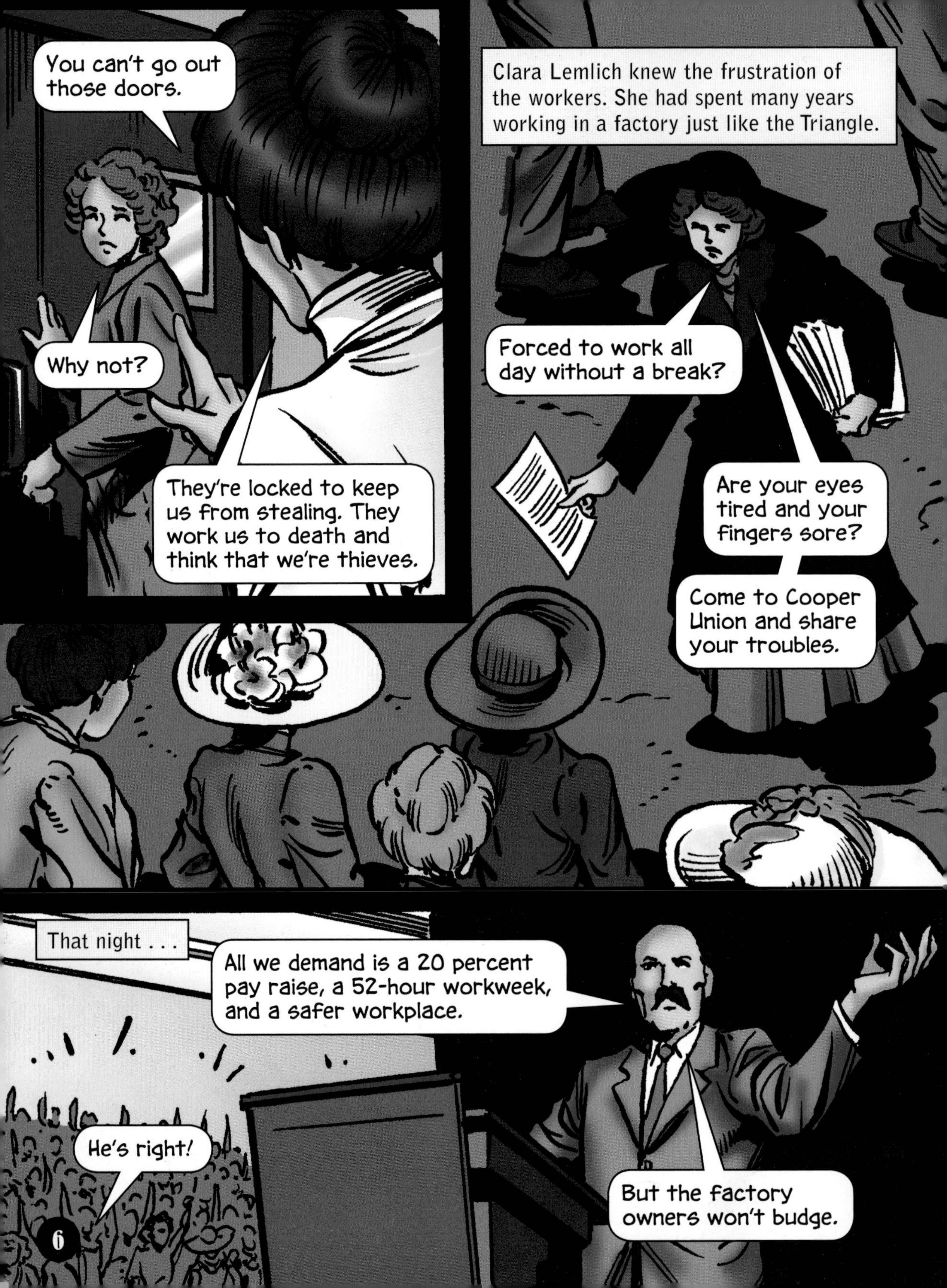
You can't go out those doors.
Why not?
They're locked to keep us from stealing. They work us to death and think that we're thieves.
Clara Lemlich knew the frustration of the workers. She had spent many years working in a factory just like the Triangle.
Forced to work all day without a break?
Are your eyes tired and your fingers sore?
Come to Cooper Union and share your troubles.
That night . . .
All we demand is a 20 percent pay raise, a 52-hour workweek, and a safer workplace.
He's right!
But the factory owners won't budge.

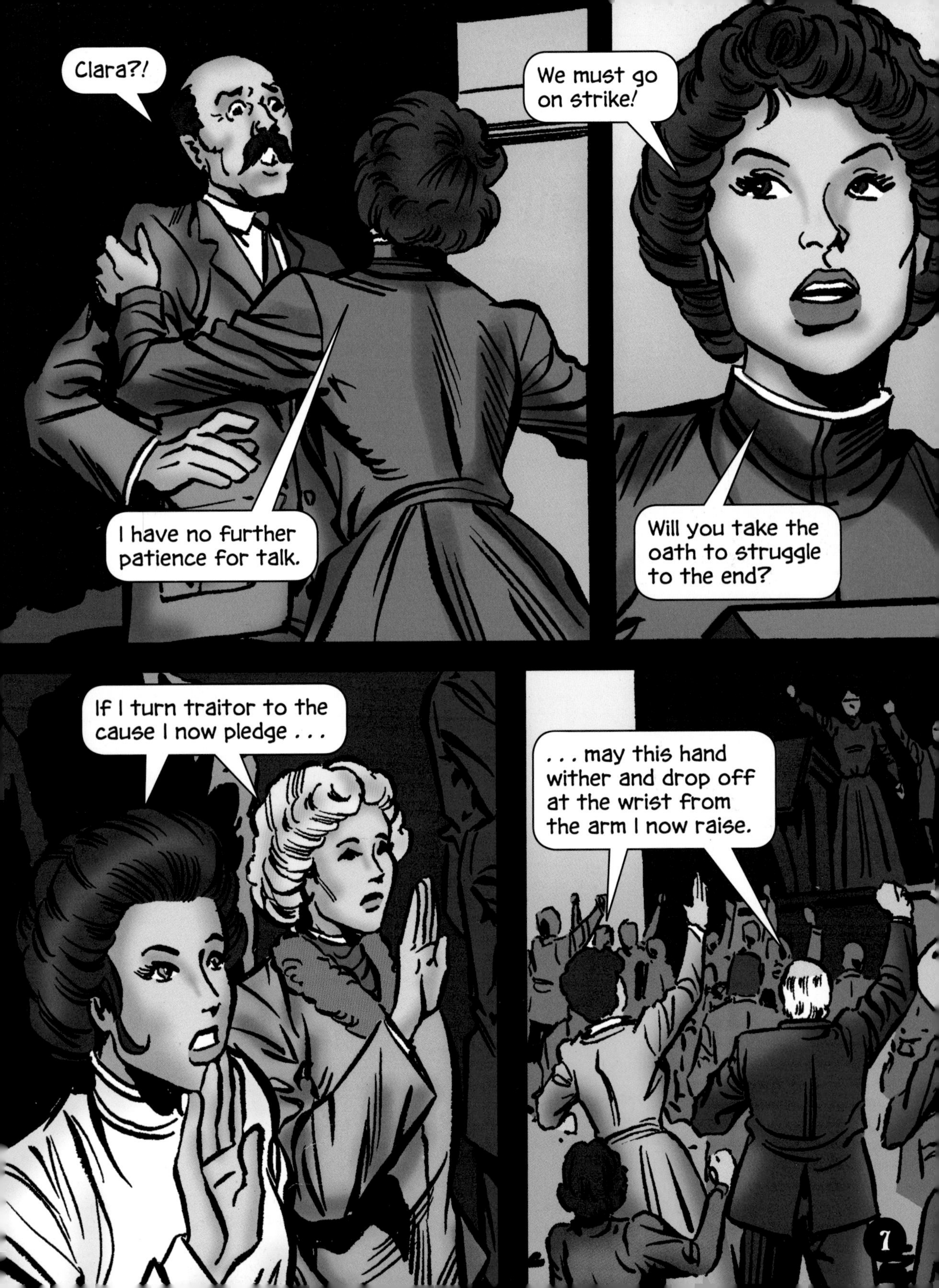
Clara?!
We must go on strike!
I have no further patience for talk.
Will you take the oath to struggle to the end?
If I turn traitor to the cause I now pledge . . .
. . . may this hand wither and drop off at the wrist from the arm I now raise.

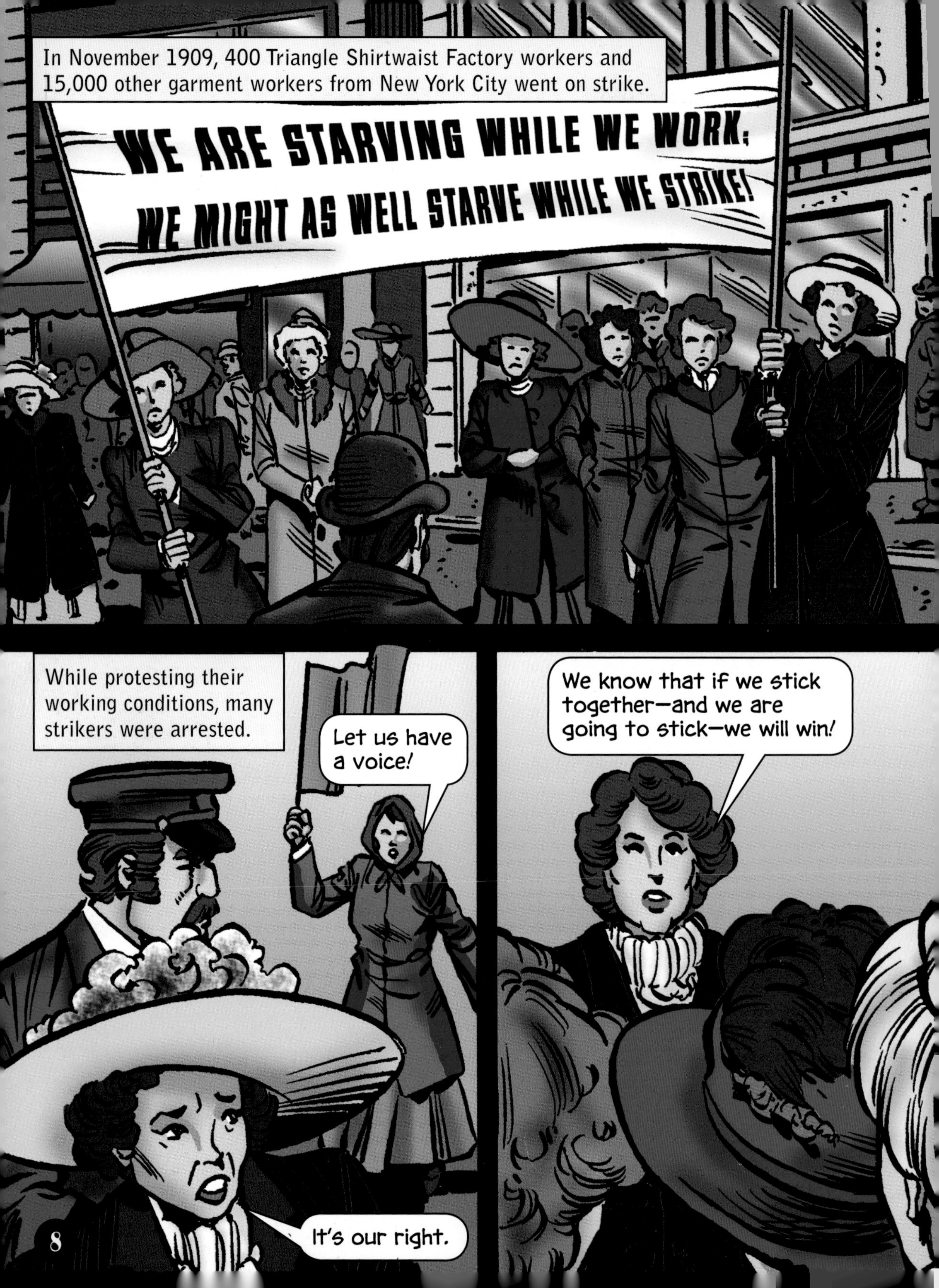
In November 1909, 400 Triangle Shirtwaist Factory workers and 15,000 other garment workers from New York City went on strike.
WE ARE STARVING WHILE WE WORK; WE MIGHT AS WELL STARVE WHILE WE STRIKE!
While protesting their working conditions, many strikers were arrested.
Let us have a voice!
It's our right.
We know that if we stick together—and we are going to stick—we will win!

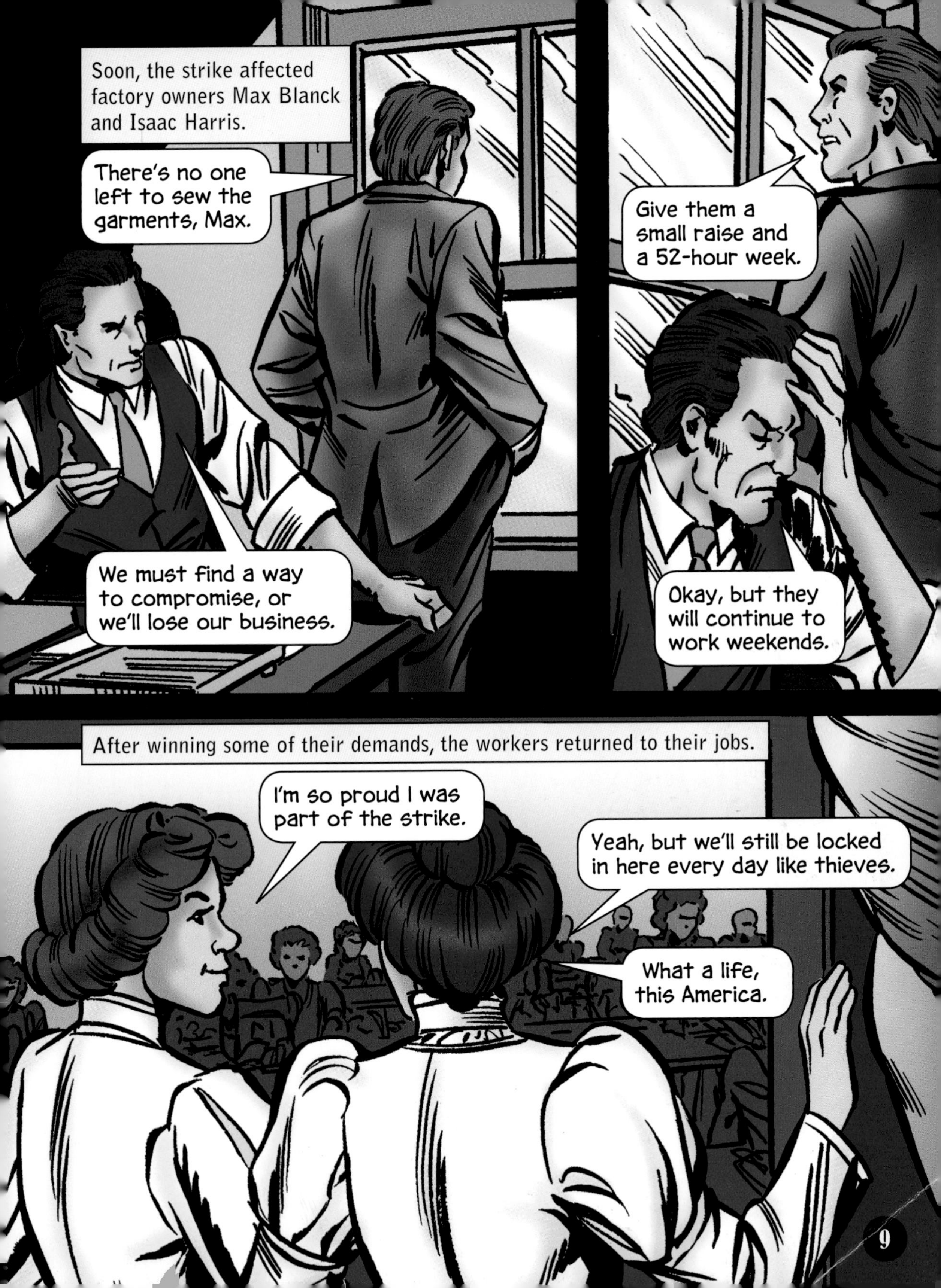

Soon, the strike affected factory owners Max Blanck and Isaac Harris.
There's no one left to sew the garments, Max.
We must find a way to compromise, or we'll lose our business.
Give them a small raise and a 52-hour week.
Okay, but they will continue to work weekends.
After winning some of their demands, the workers returned to their jobs.
I'm so proud I was part of the strike.
Yeah, but we'll still be locked in here every day like thieves.
What a life, this America.

Chapter 2
TRAPPED IN FLAMES

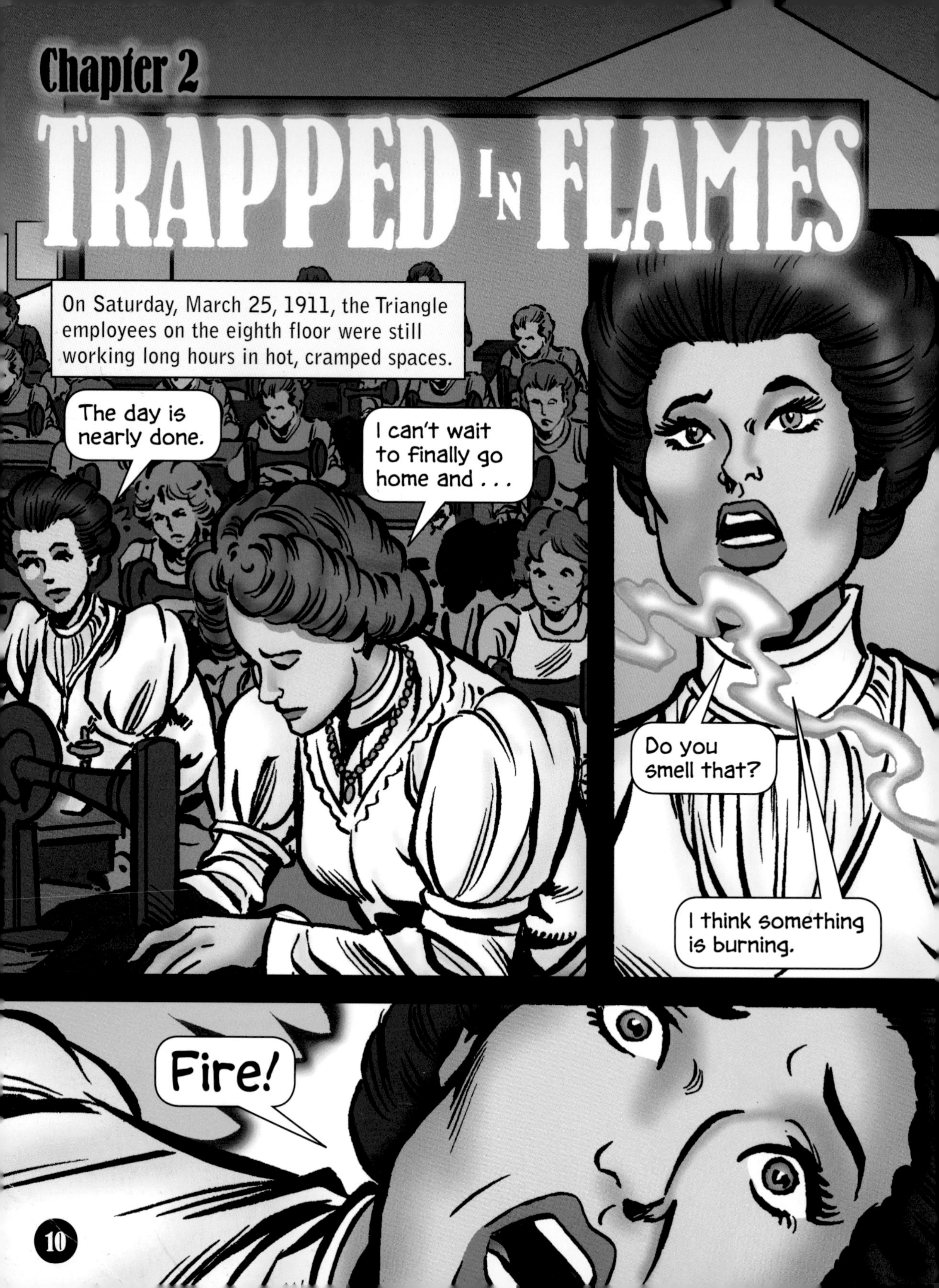
On Saturday, March 25, 1911, the Triangle employees on the eighth floor were still working long hours in hot, cramped spaces.
The day is nearly done.
I can't wait to finally go home and . . .
Do you smell that?
I think something is burning.
Fire!

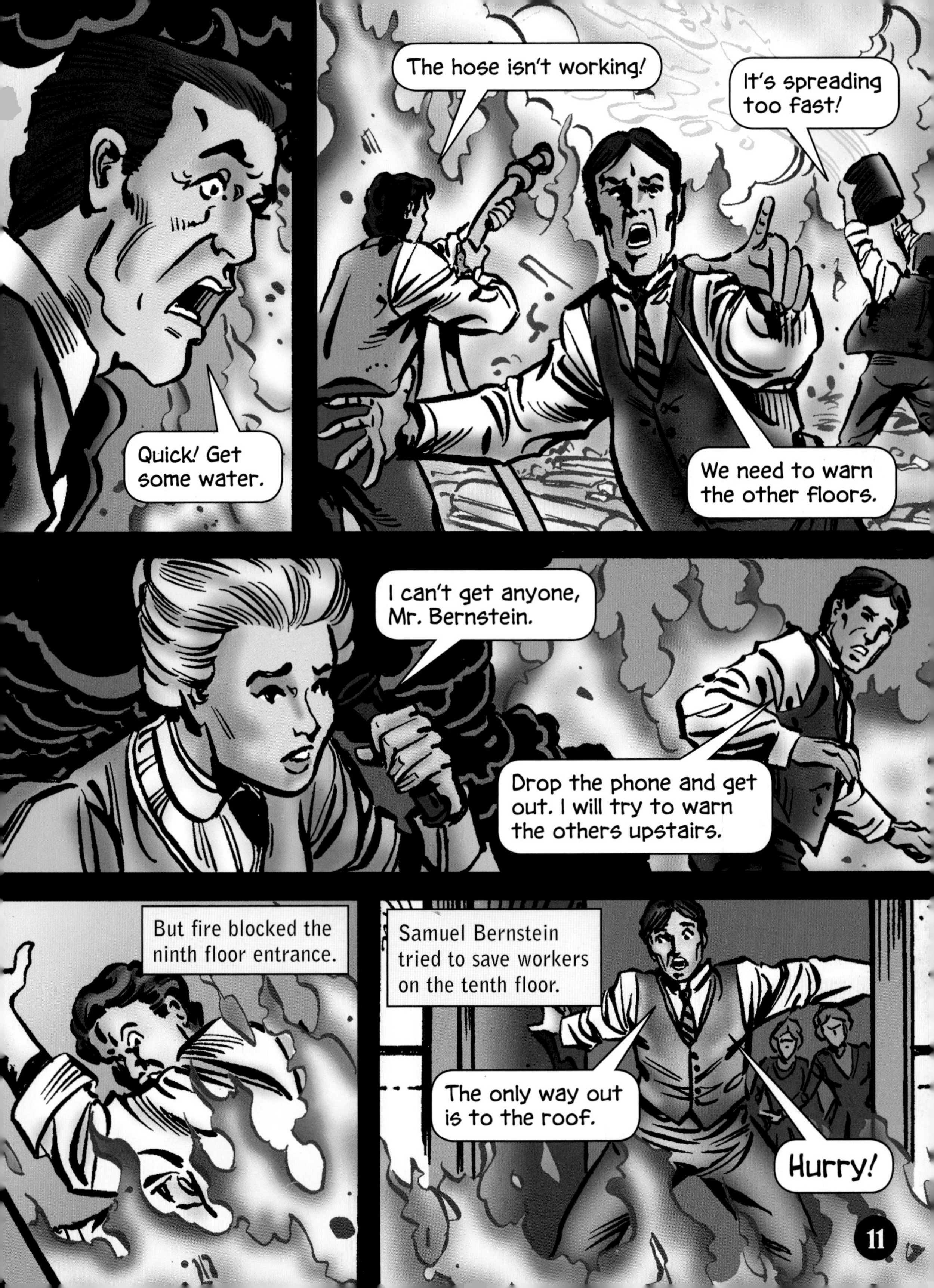

Quick! Get some water.
The hose isn't working!
It's spreading too fast!
We need to warn the other floors.
I can't get anyone, Mr. Bernstein.
Drop the phone and get out. I will try to warn the others upstairs.
But fire blocked the ninth floor entrance.
Samuel Bernstein tried to save workers on the tenth floor.
The only way out is to the roof.
Hurry!

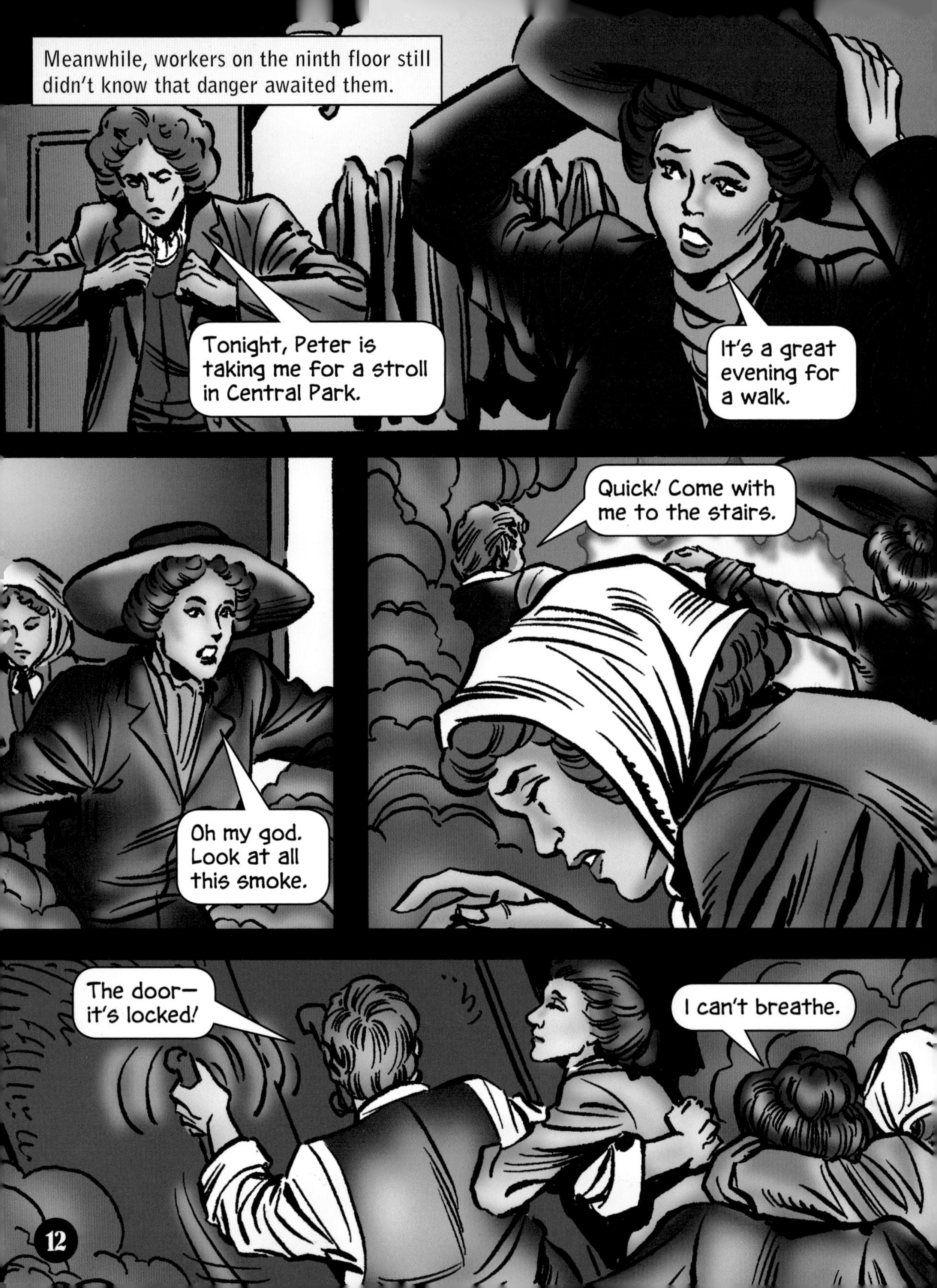
Meanwhile, workers on the ninth floor still didn't know that danger awaited them.
Tonight, Peter is taking me for a stroll in Central Park.
It's a great evening for a walk.
Oh my god. Look at all this smoke.
Quick! Come with me to the stairs.
The door— it's locked!
I can't breathe.

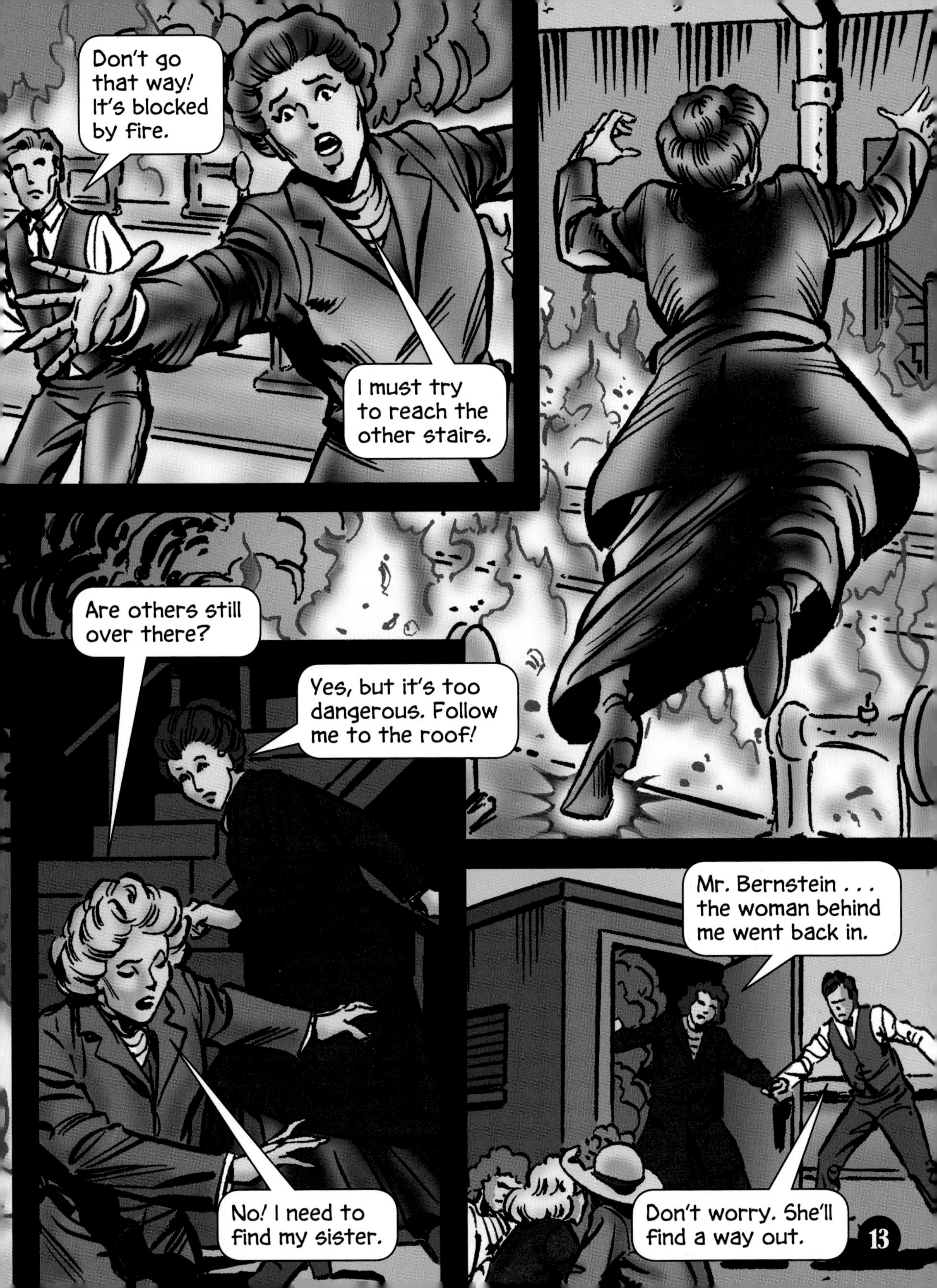
Don't go that way! It's blocked by fire.
I must try to reach the other stairs.
Are others still over there?
Yes, but it's too dangerous. Follow me to the roof!
No! I need to find my sister.
Mr. Bernstein . . . the woman behind me went back in.
Don't worry. She'll find a way out.

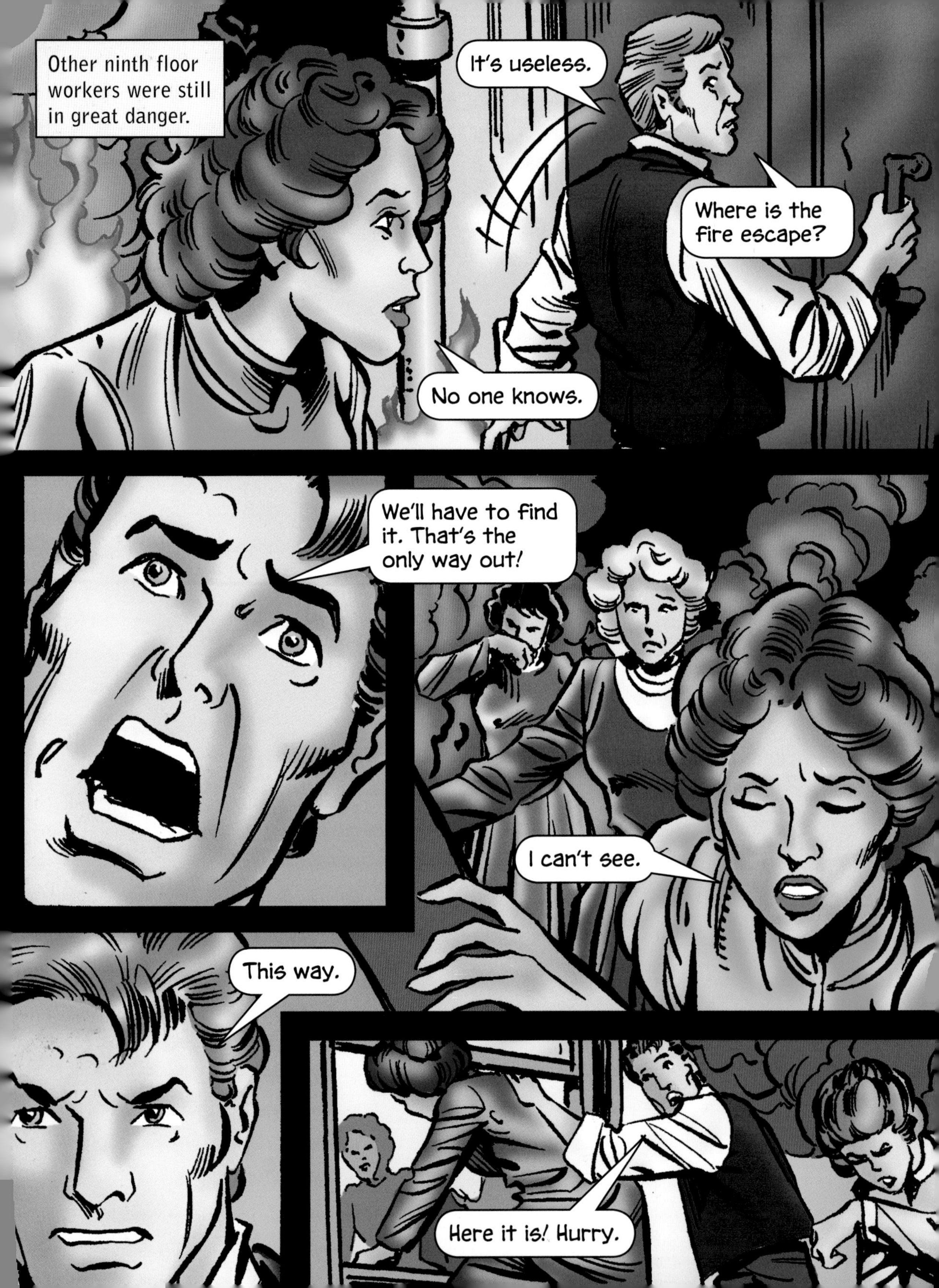
Other ninth floor workers were still in great danger.
It's useless.
Where is the fire escape?
No one knows.
We'll have to find it. That's the only way out!
I can't see.
This way.
Here it is! Hurry.

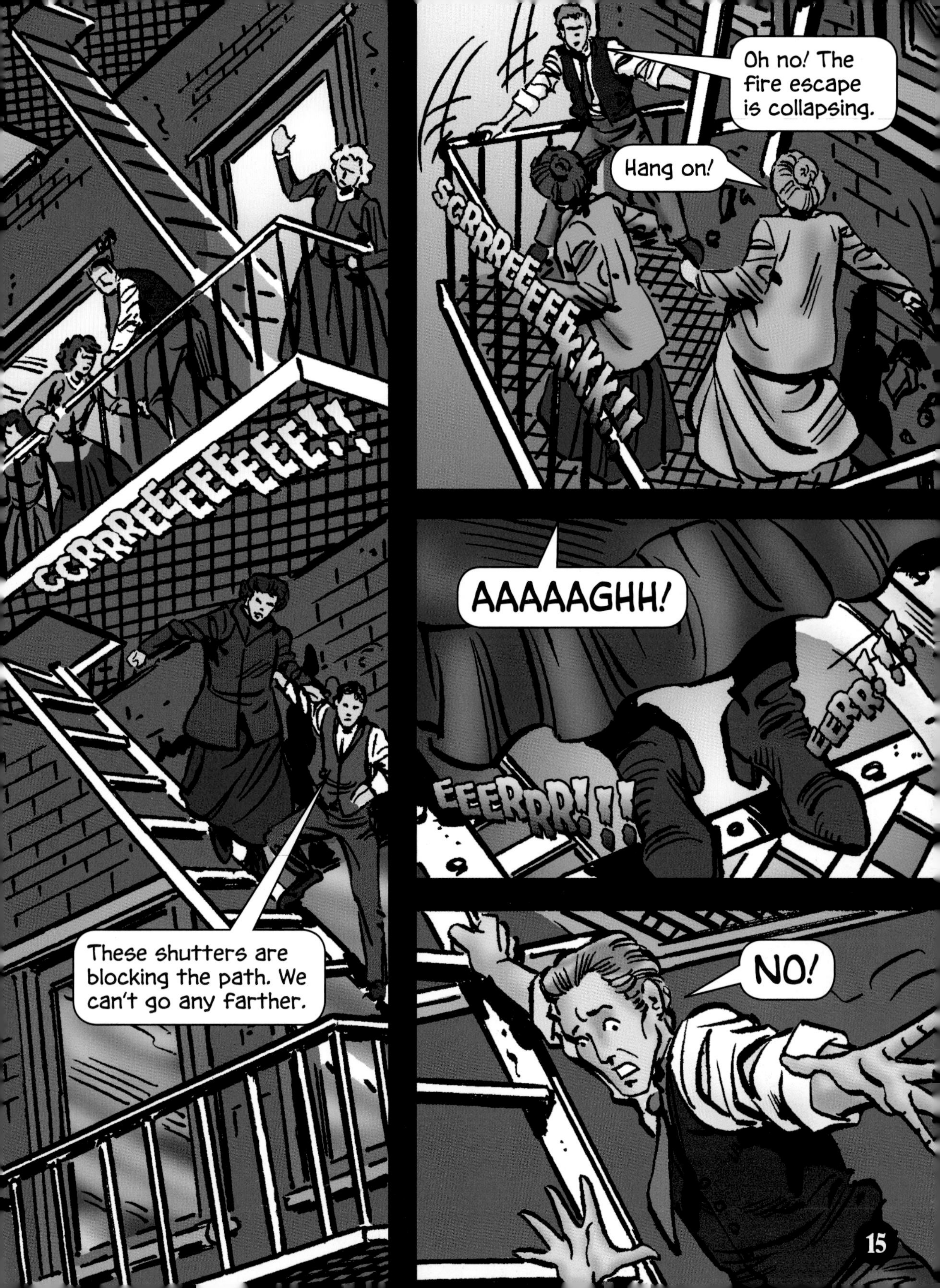

GGRRREEEEEEEEE!!
These shutters are blocking the path. We can't go any farther.
Oh no! The fire escape is collapsing.
Hang on!
SCRRREEEEEKKK!!
AAAAAGHH!
EERR!!!
EEERRR!!!
NO!

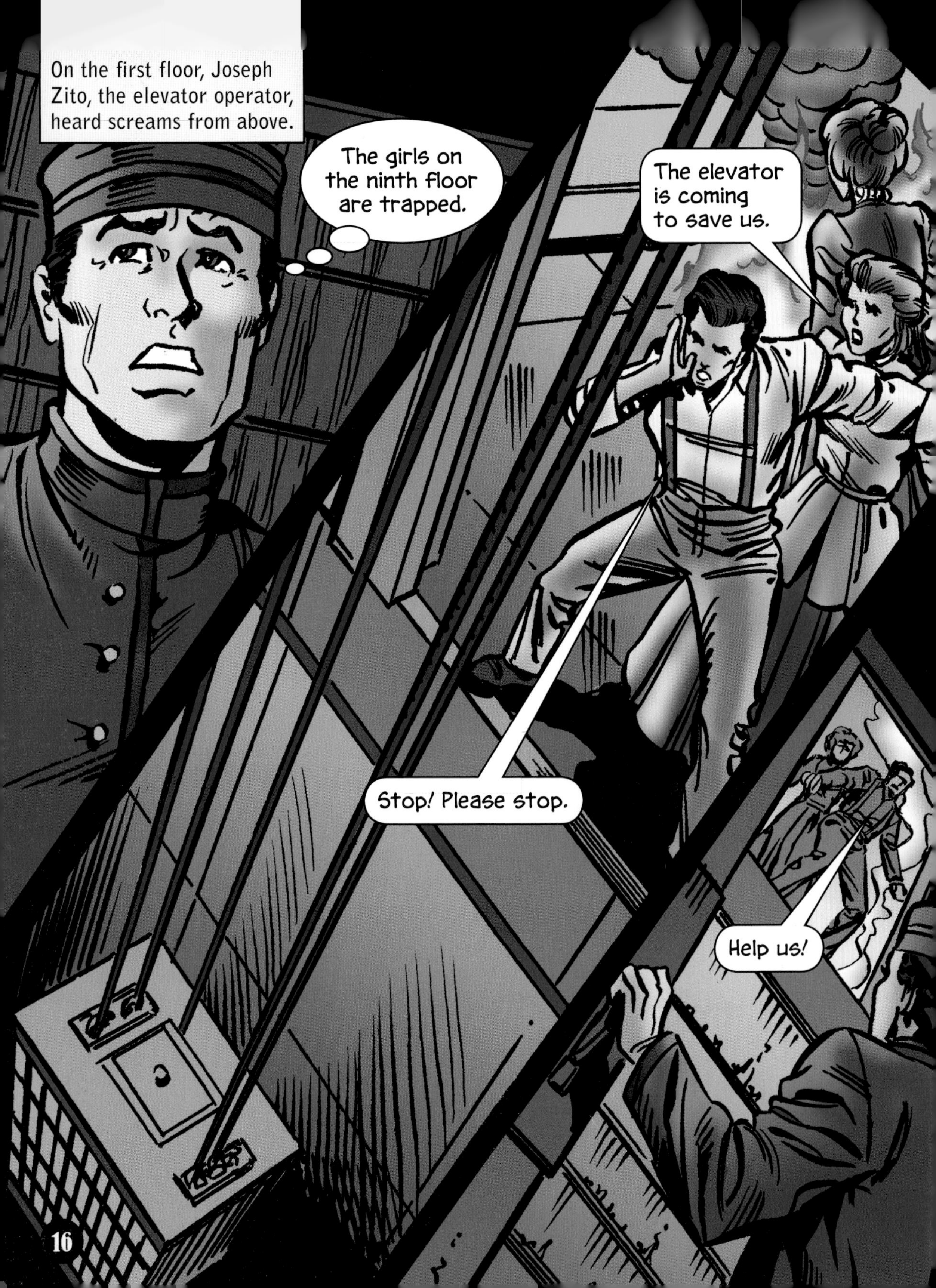
On the first floor, Joseph Zito, the elevator operator, heard screams from above.
The girls on the ninth floor are trapped.
The elevator is coming to save us.
Stop! Please stop.
Help us!

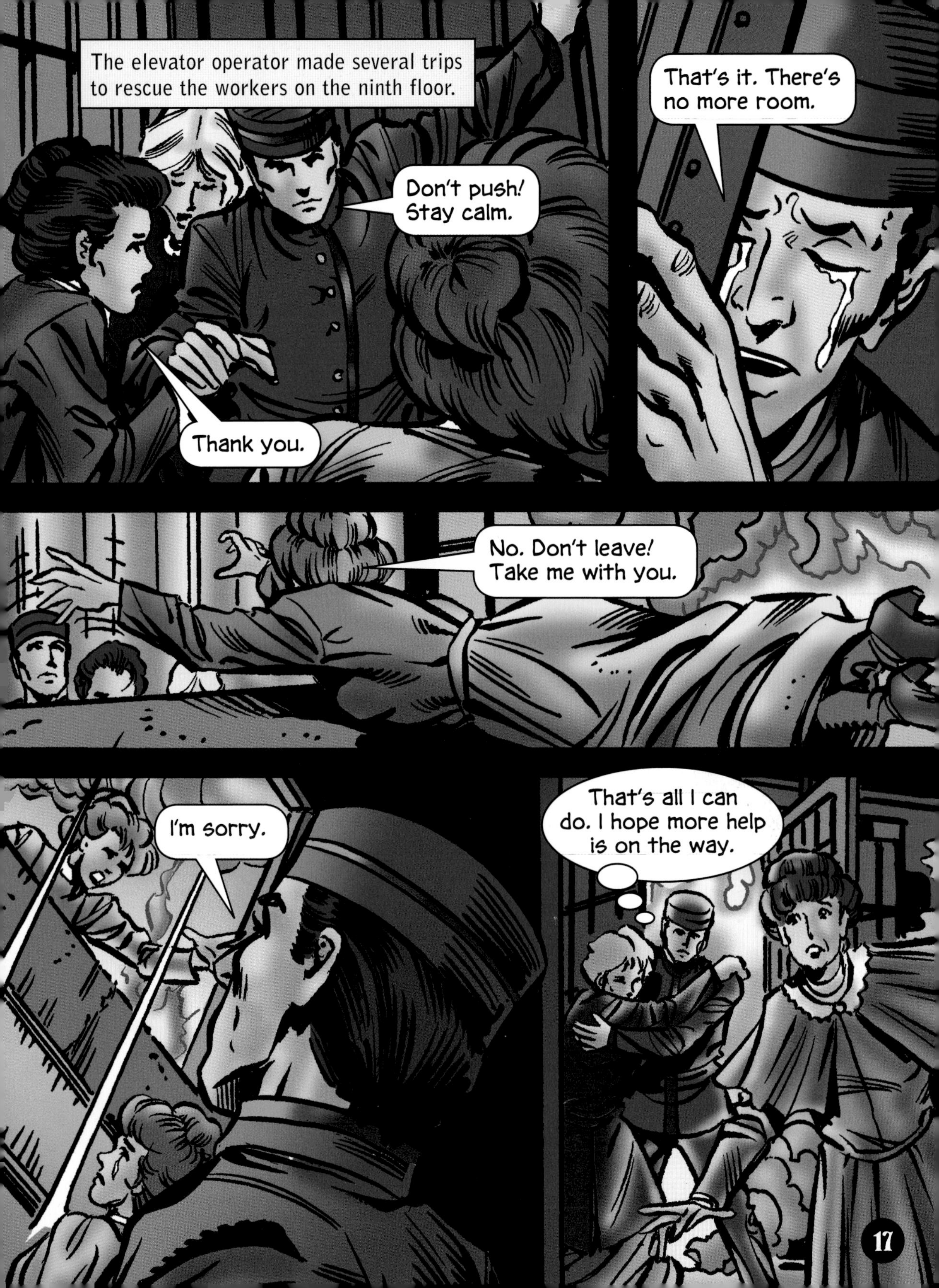
The elevator operator made several trips to rescue the workers on the ninth floor.
Don't push! Stay calm.
Thank you.
That's it. There's no more room.
No. Don't leave! Take me with you.
I'm sorry.
That's all I can do. I hope more help is on the way.

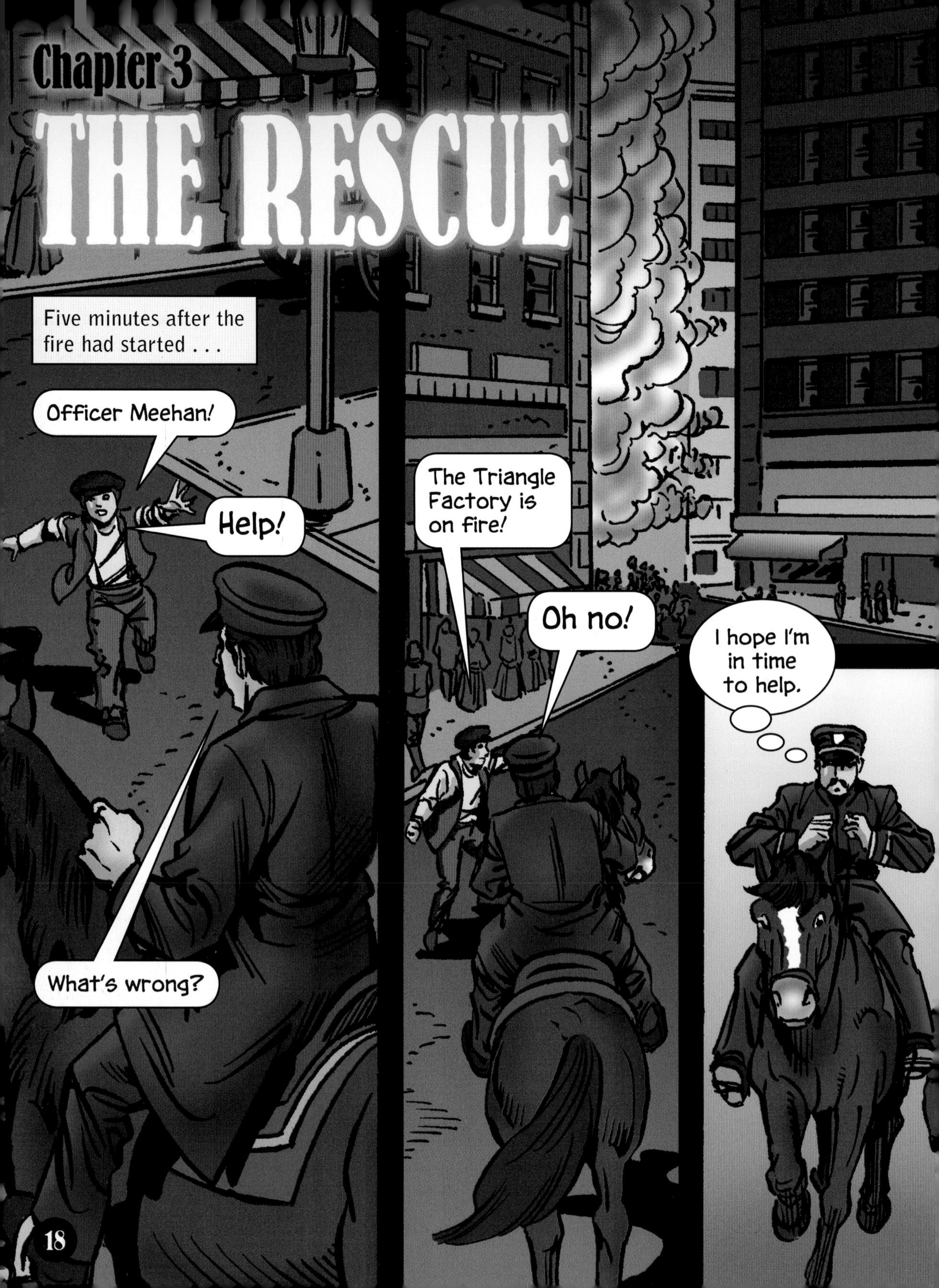
Chapter 3
THE RESCUE
Five minutes after the fire had started . . .
Officer Meehan!
Help!
What's wrong?
The Triangle Factory is on fire!
Oh no!
I hope I'm in time to help.

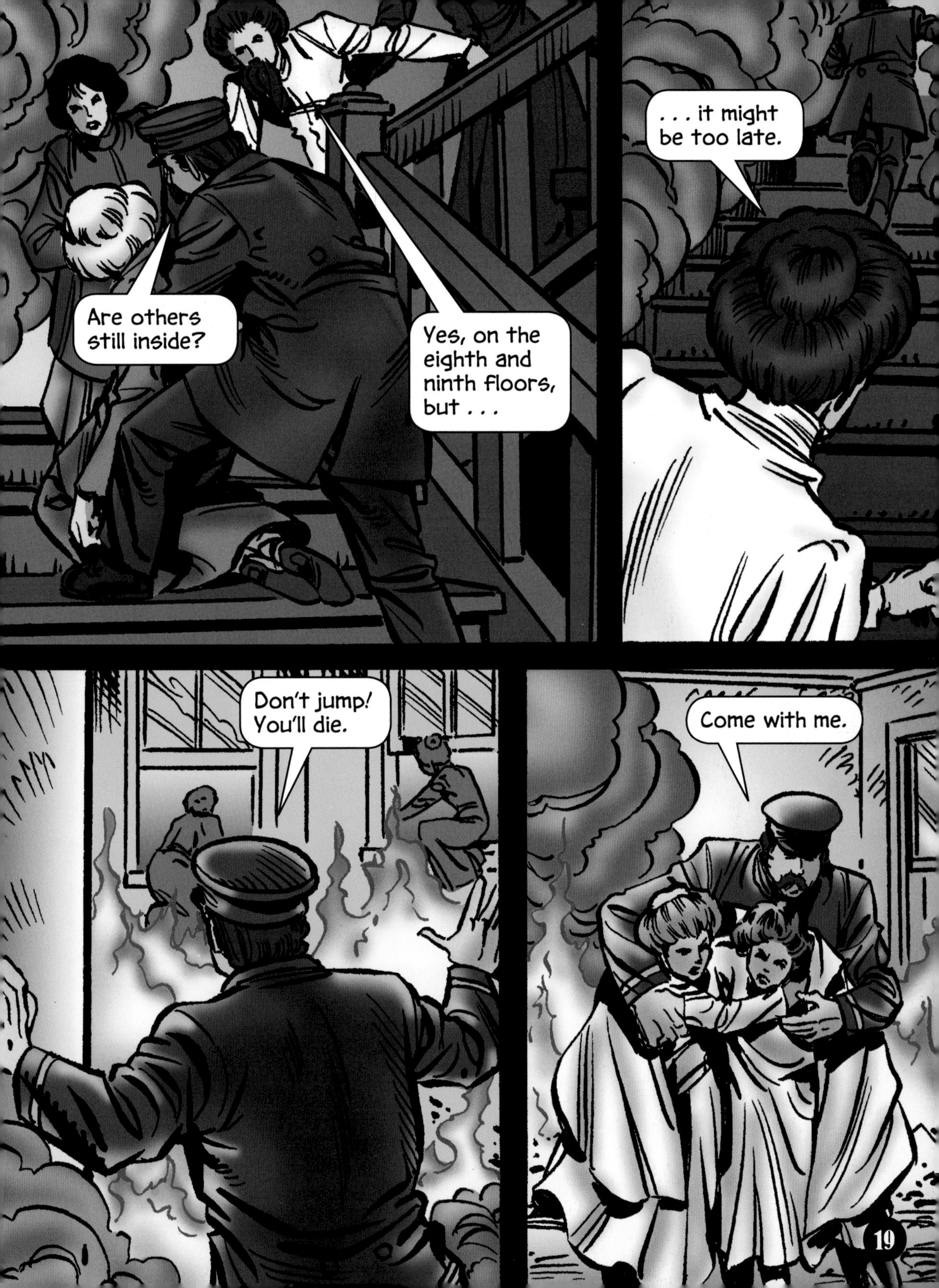
Are others still inside?
Yes, on the eighth and ninth floors, but . . .
. . . it might be too late.
Don't jump! You'll die.
Come with me.

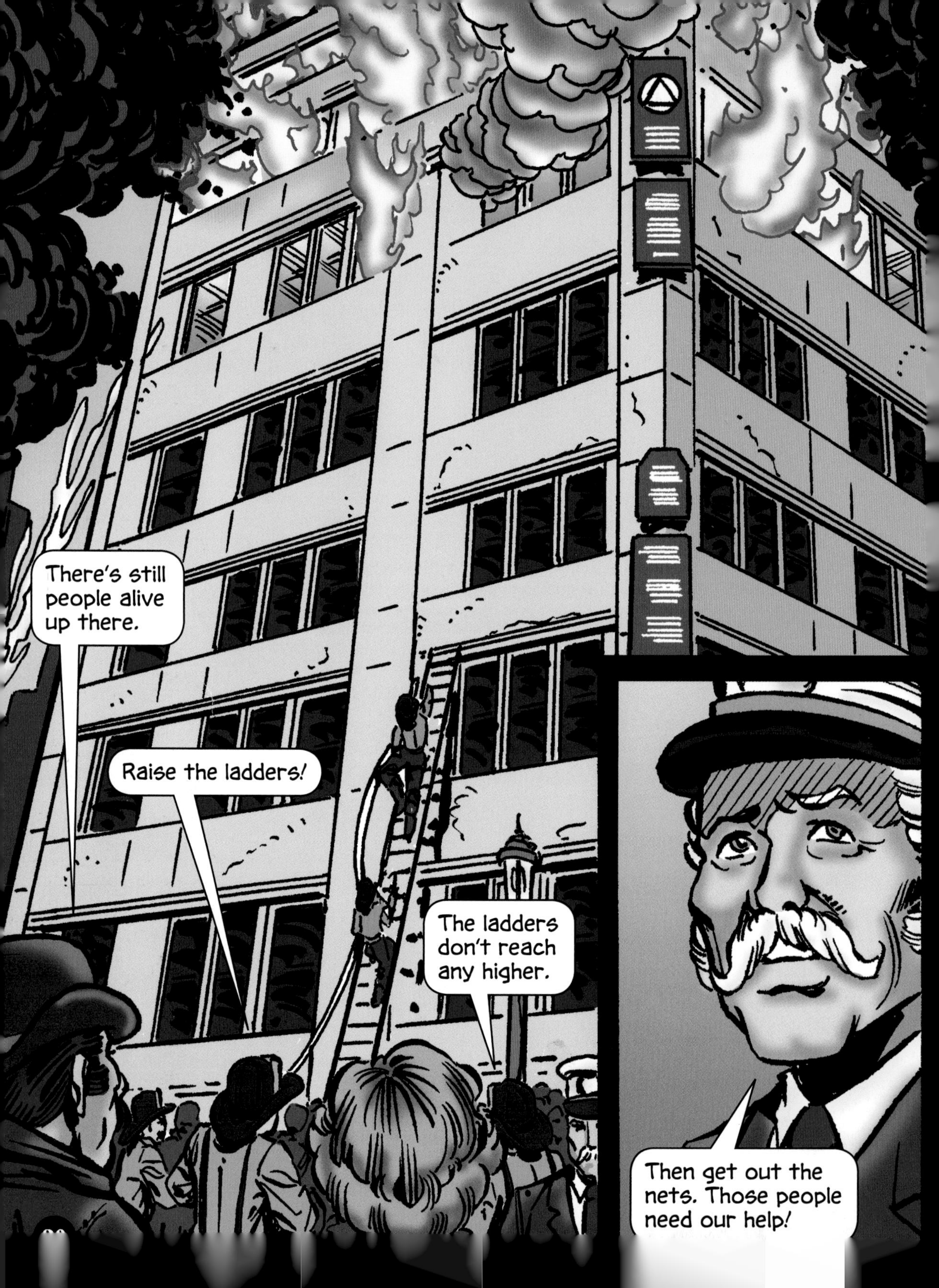
There's still people alive up there.
Raise the ladders!
The ladders don't reach any higher.
Then get out the nets. Those people need our help!

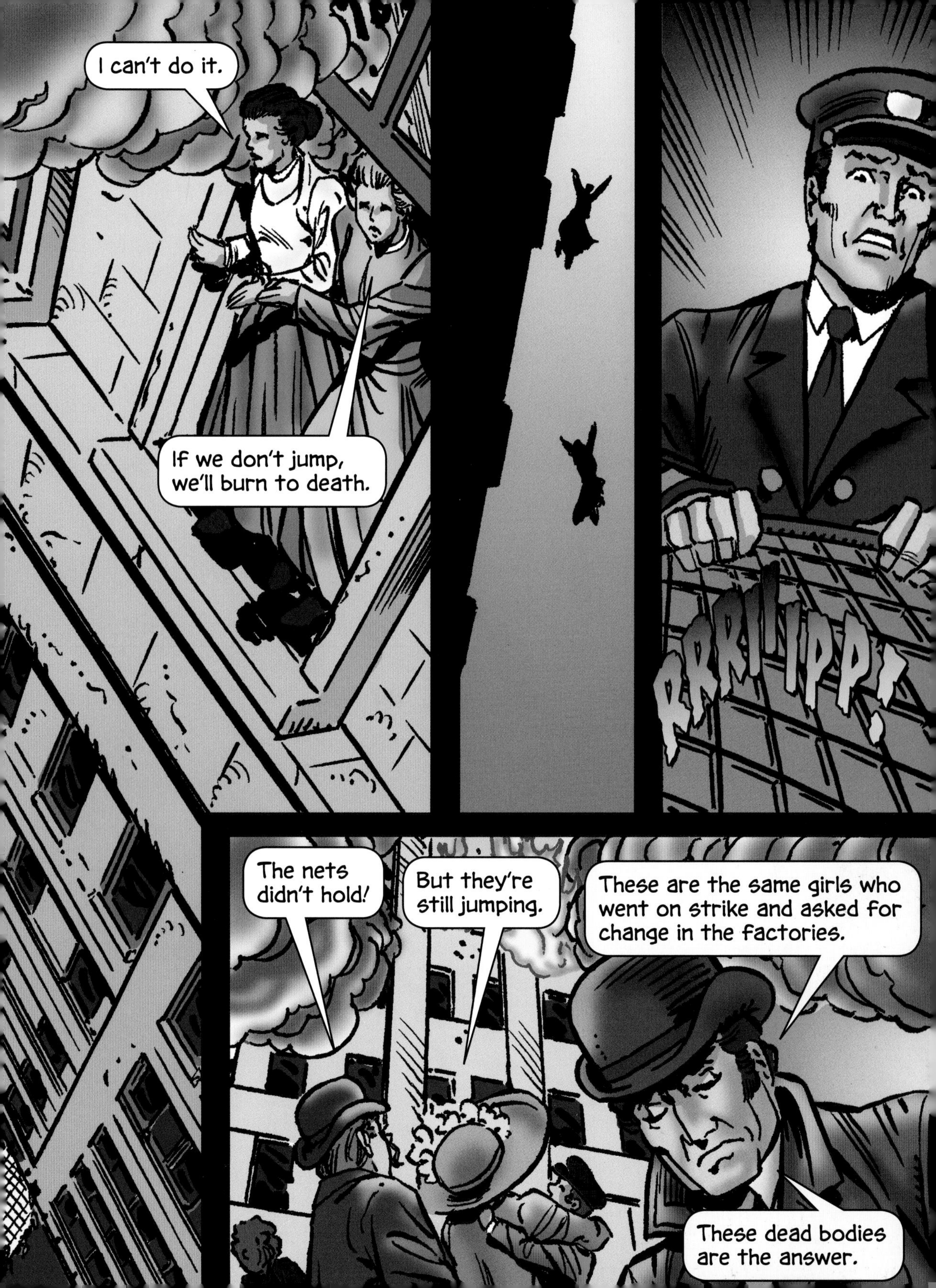
I can't do it.
If we don't jump, we'll burn to death.
RRRIIIPP!
The nets didn't hold!
But they're still jumping.
These are the same girls who went on strike and asked for change in the factories.
These dead bodies are the answer.

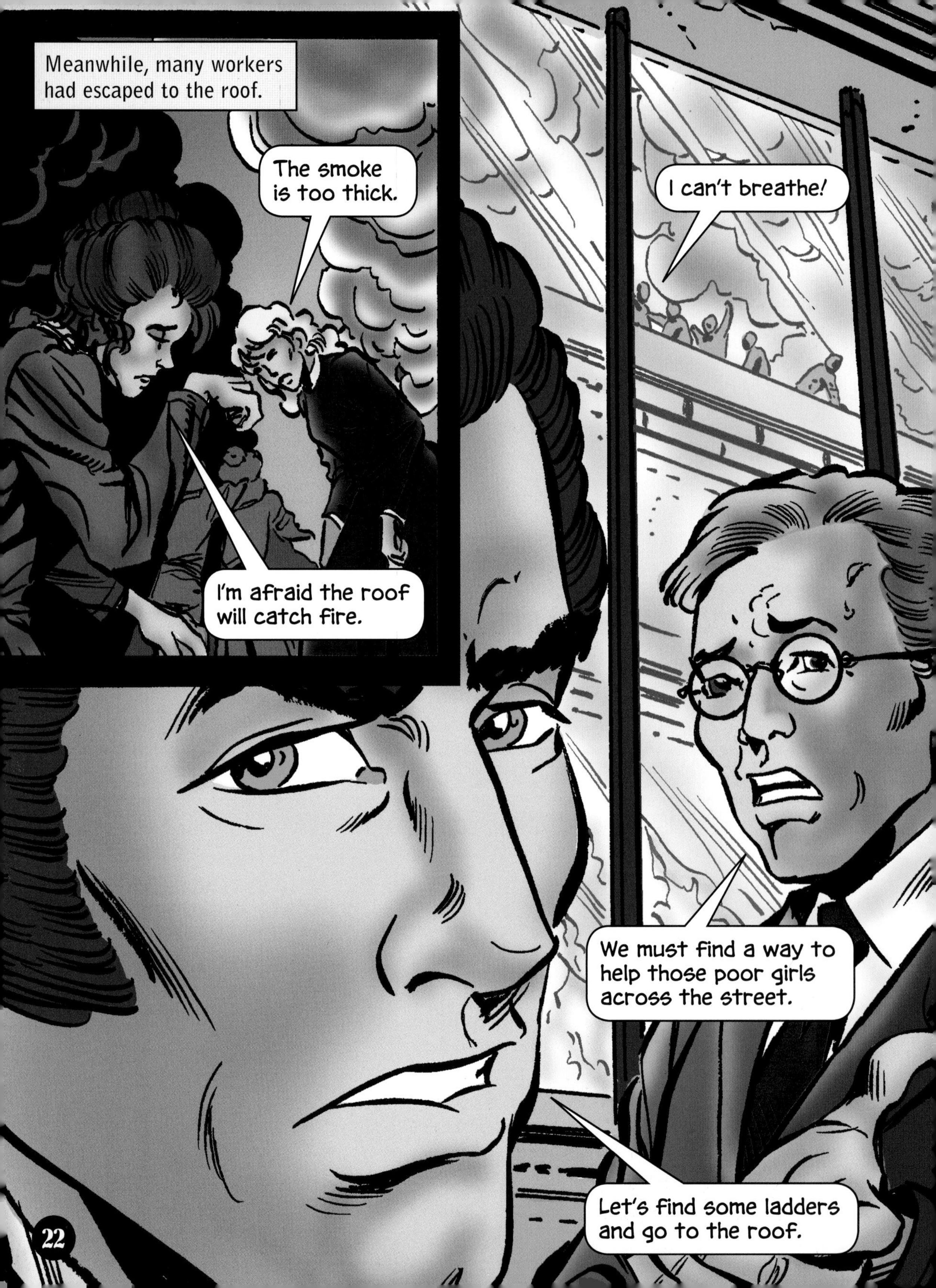
Meanwhile, many workers had escaped to the roof.
The smoke is too thick.
I'm afraid the roof will catch fire.
I can't breathe!
We must find a way to help those poor girls across the street.
Let's find some ladders and go to the roof.

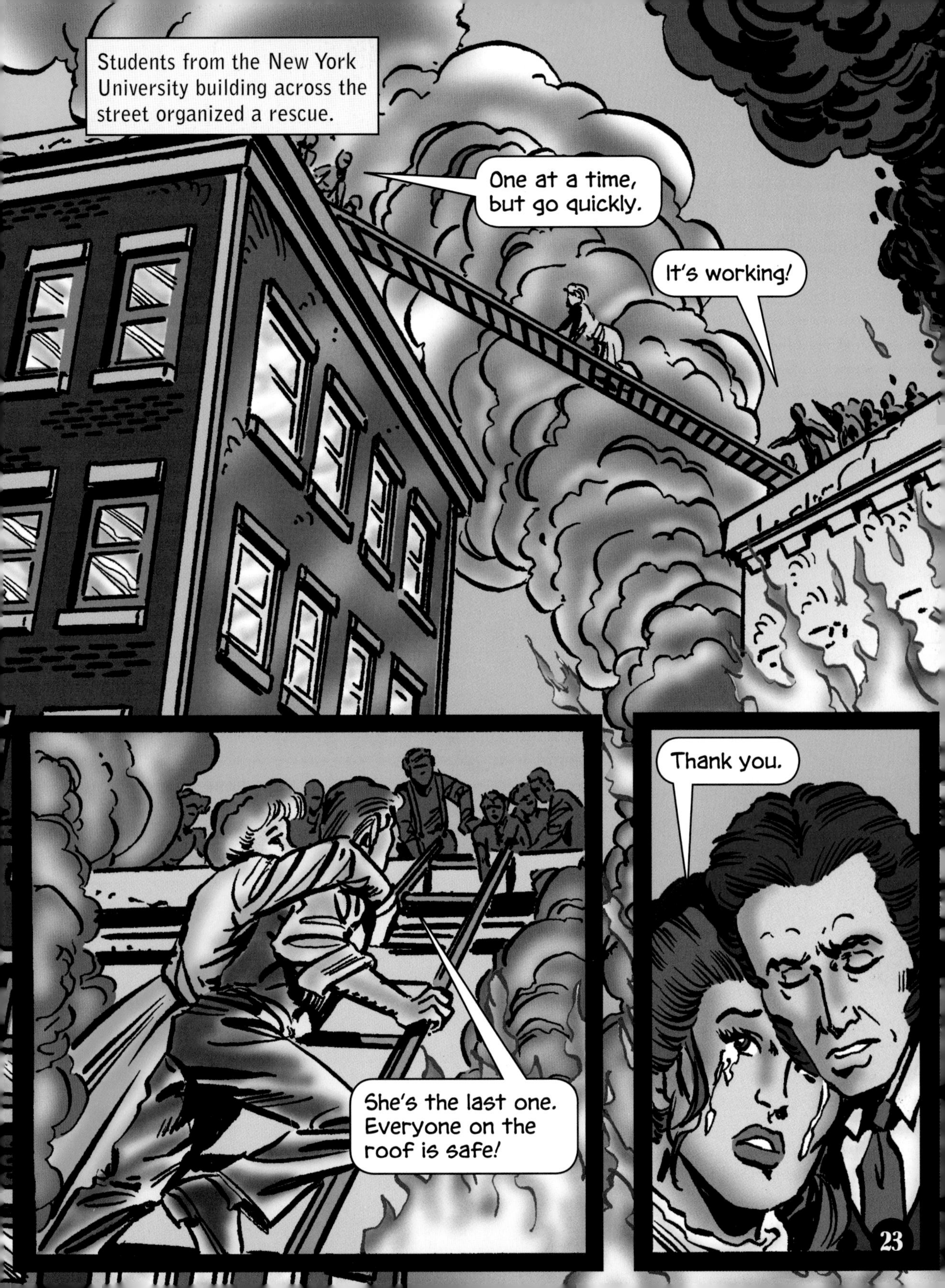
Students from the New York University building across the street organized a rescue.
One at a time, but go quickly.
It's working!
She's the last one. Everyone on the roof is safe!
Thank you.

Chapter 4
FROM THE ASHES

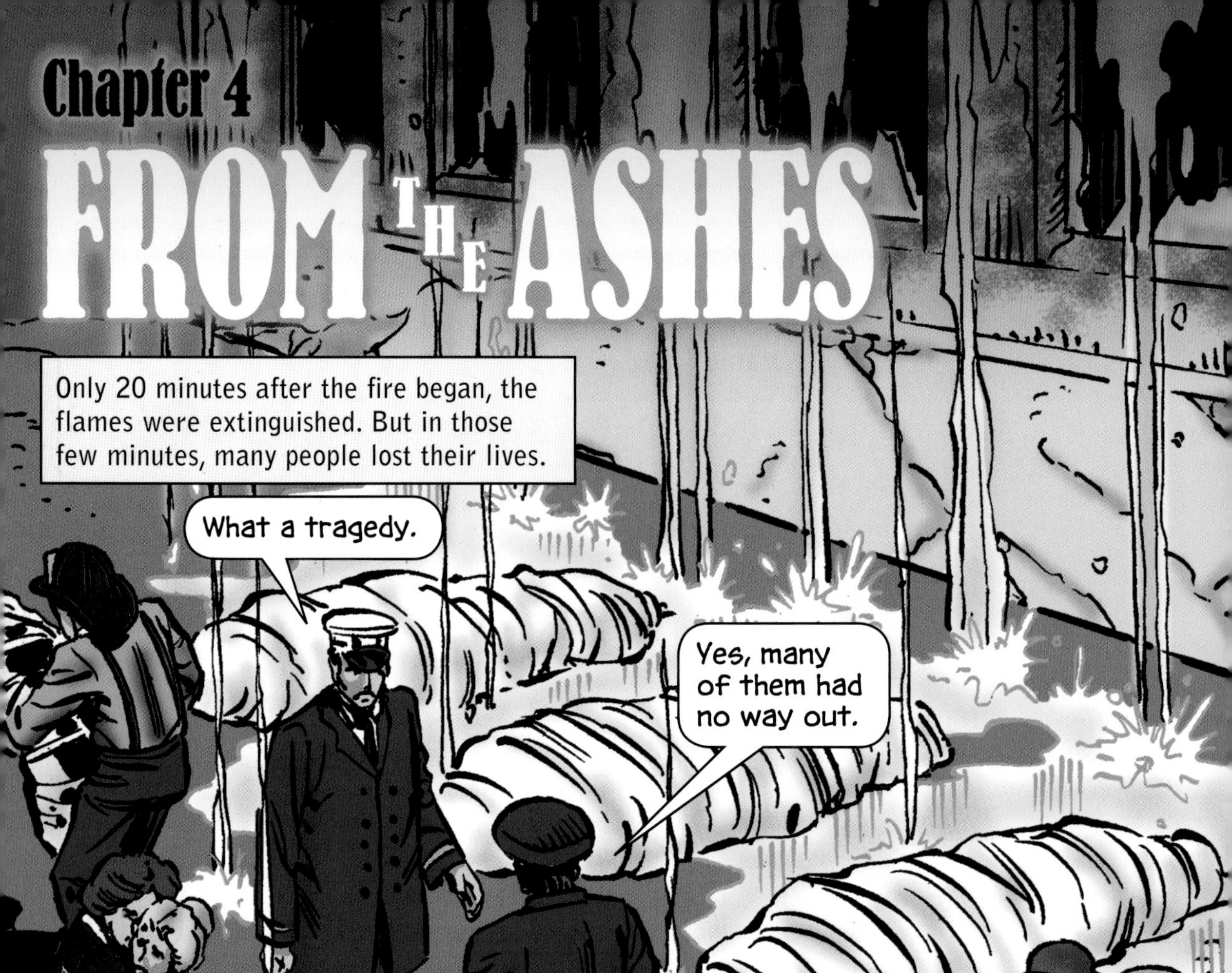

Only 20 minutes after the fire began, the flames were extinguished. But in those few minutes, many people lost their lives.
What a tragedy.
Yes, many of them had no way out.

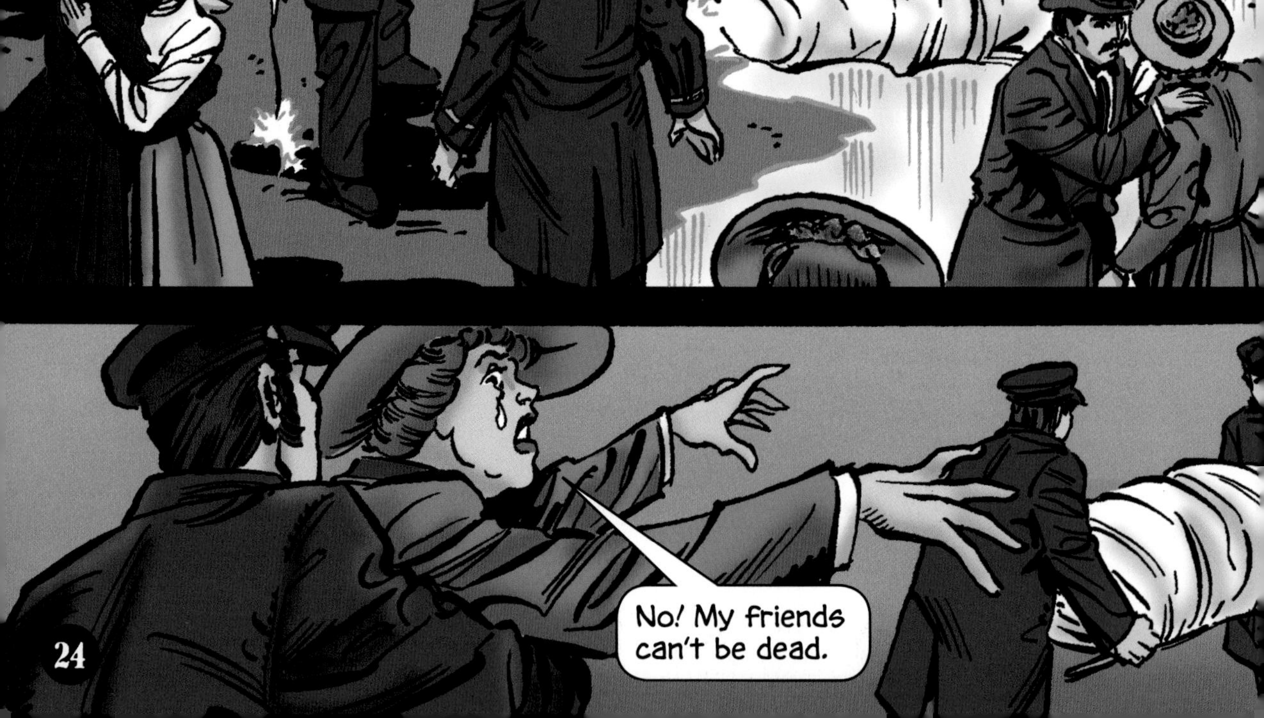

No! My friends can't be dead.

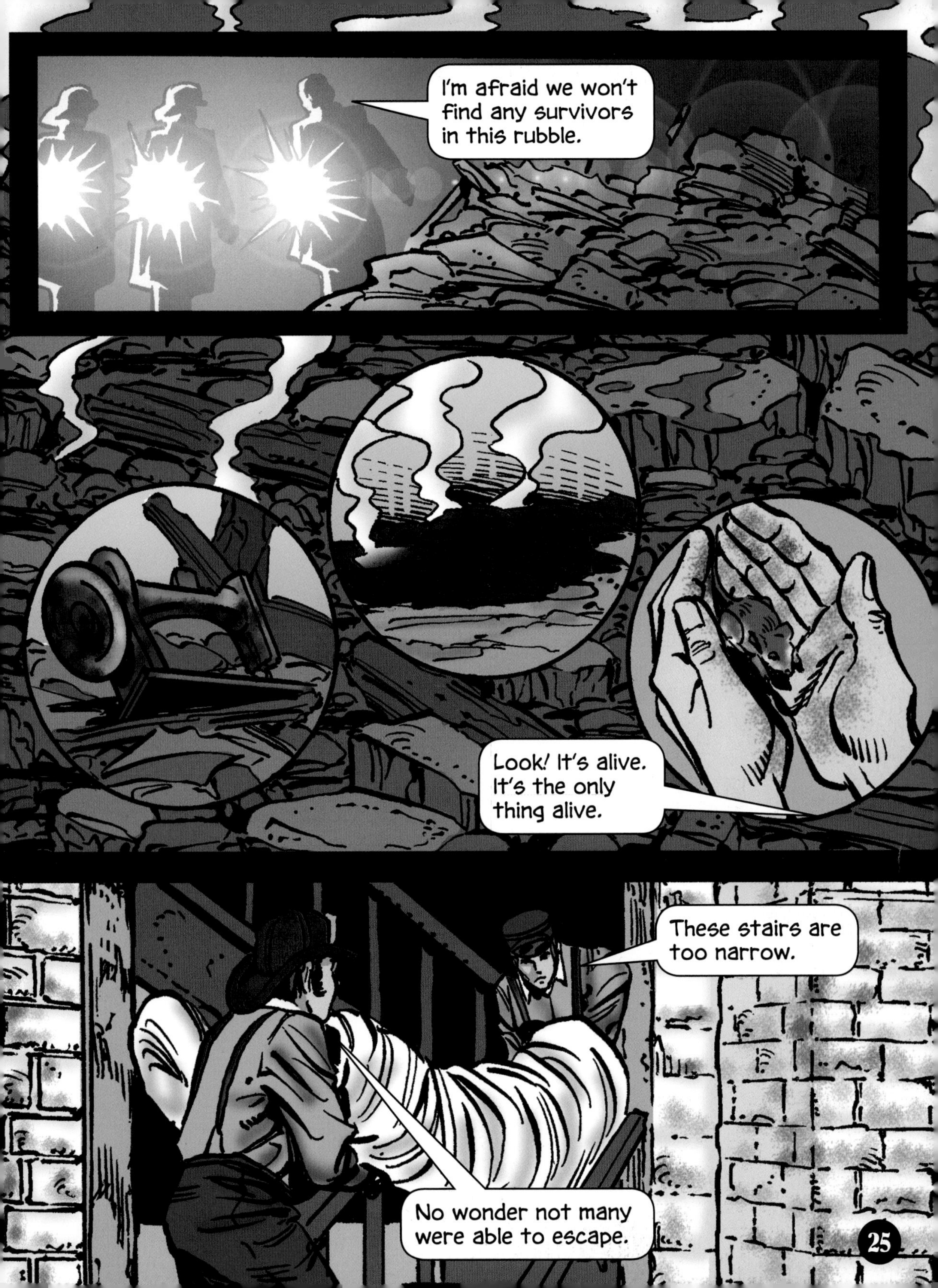
I'm afraid we won't find any survivors in this rubble.
Look! It's alive. It's the only thing alive.
These stairs are too narrow.
No wonder not many were able to escape.

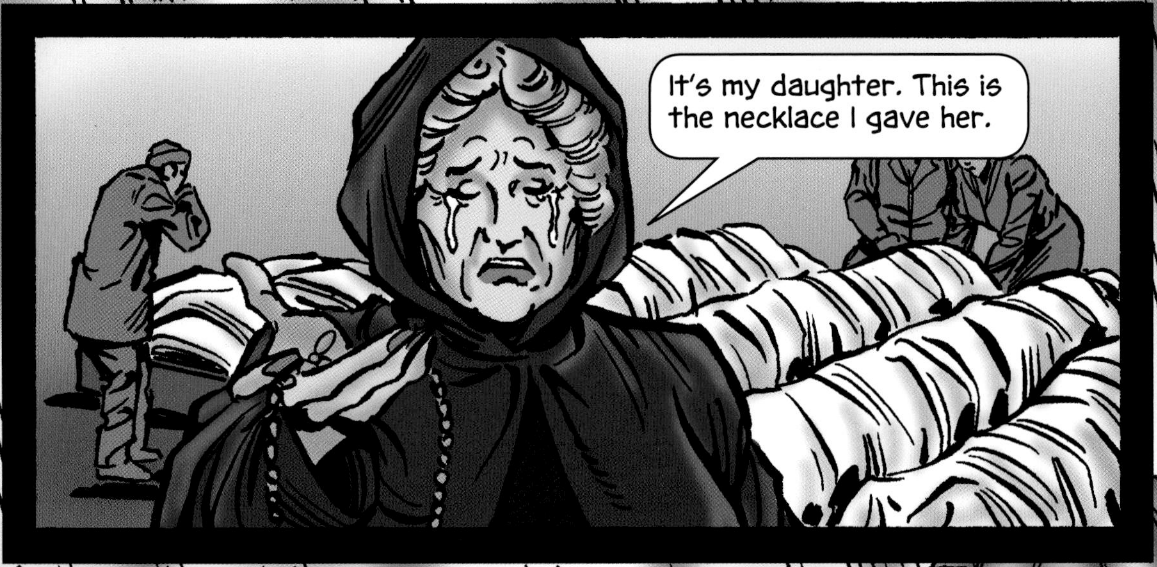
It's my daughter. This is the necklace I gave her.

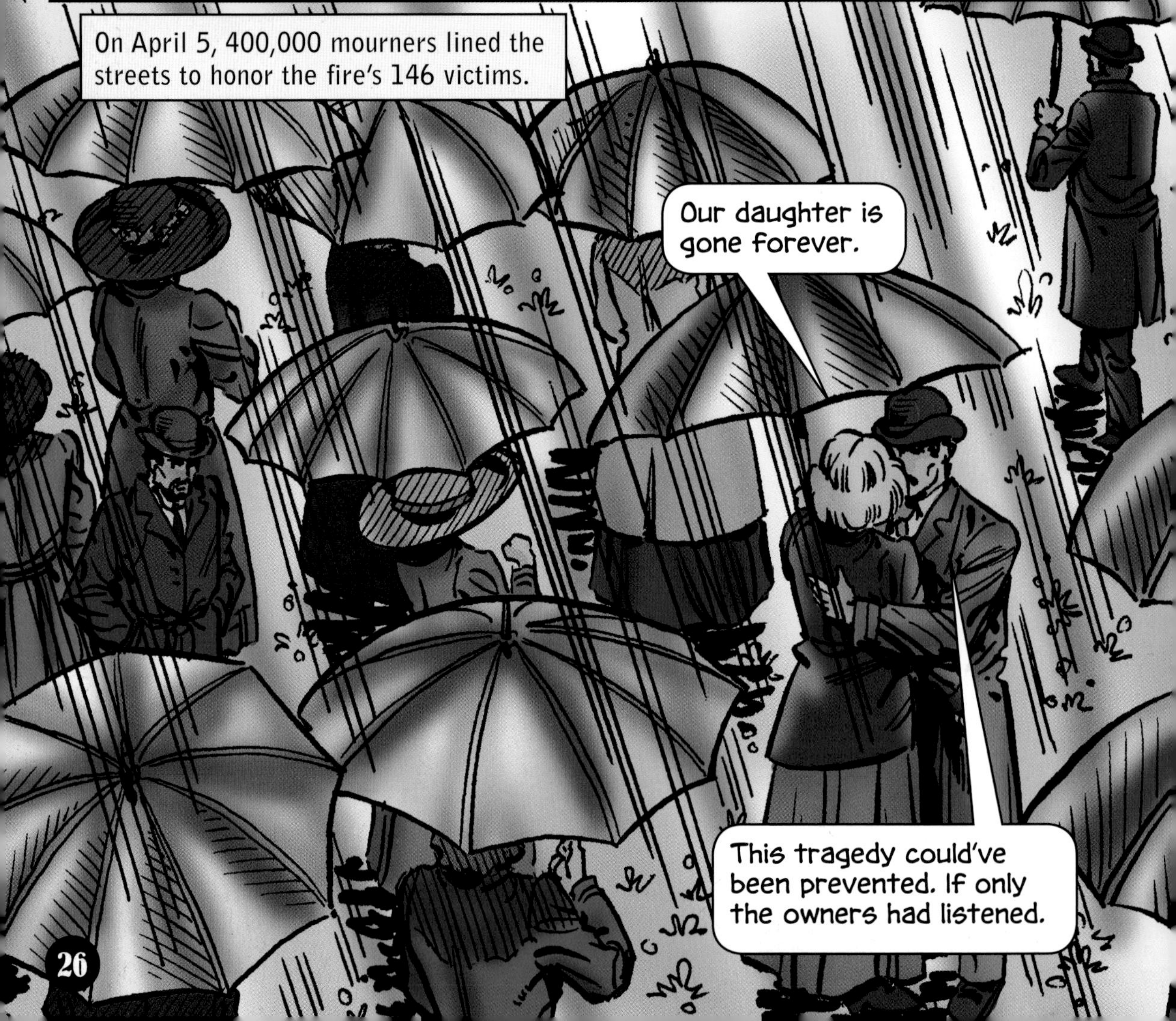
On April 5, 400,000 mourners lined the streets to honor the fire's 146 victims.
Our daughter is gone forever.
This tragedy could've been prevented. If only the owners had listened.

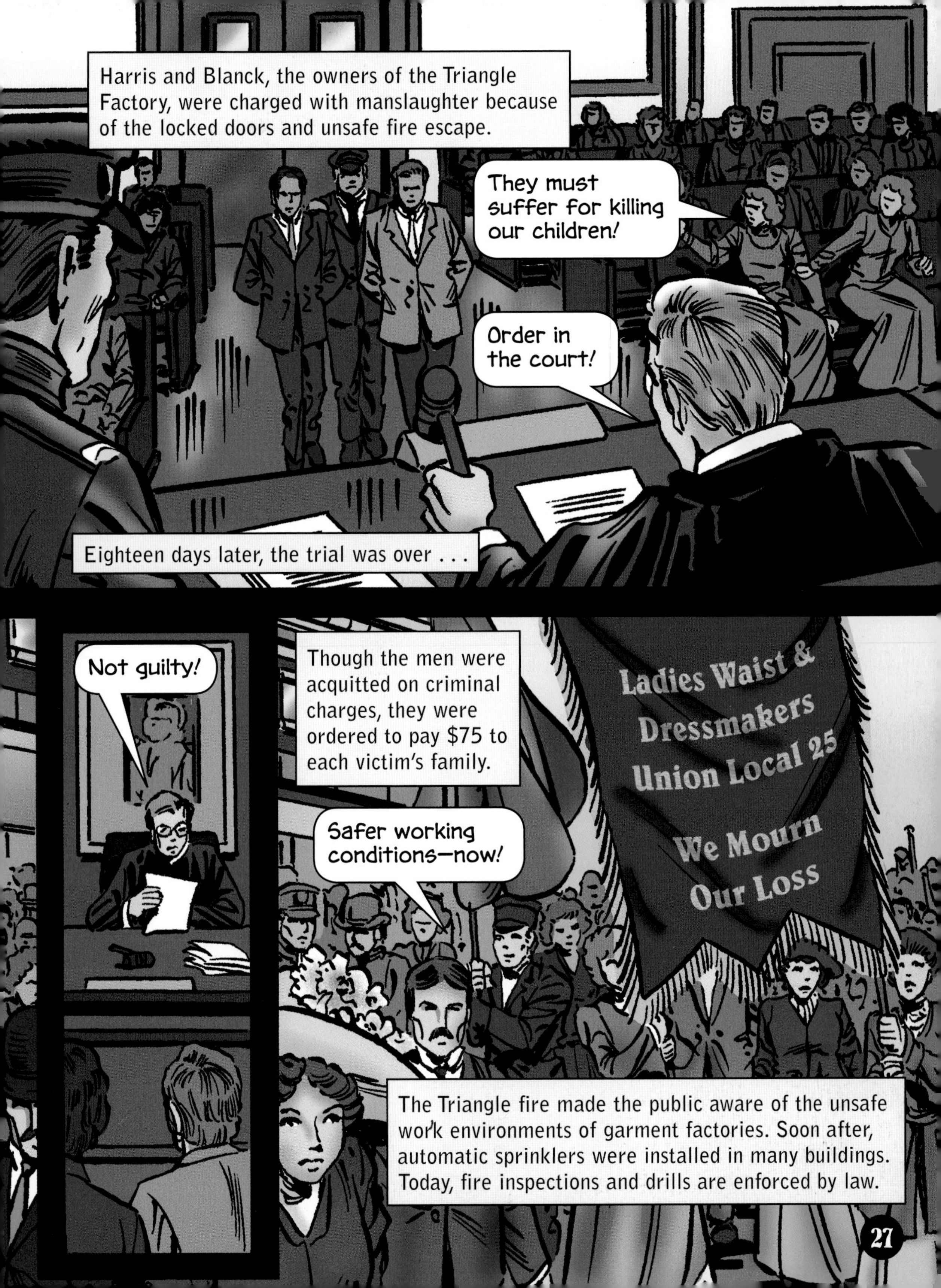

Harris and Blanck, the owners of the Triangle Factory, were charged with manslaughter because of the locked doors and unsafe fire escape.
They must suffer for killing our children!
Order in the court!
Eighteen days later, the trial was over . . .
Not guilty!
Though the men were acquitted on criminal charges, they were ordered to pay $75 to each victim's family.
Ladies Waist & Dressmakers Union Local 25
We Mourn Our Loss
Safer working conditions—now!
The Triangle fire made the public aware of the unsafe work environments of garment factories. Soon after, automatic sprinklers were installed in many buildings. Today, fire inspections and drills are enforced by law.

MORE ABOUT THE
TRIANGLE FIRE

No one knows what caused the Triangle Shirtwaist Factory fire of 1911. Some people believe a match or lit cigar ignited a pile of rags on the eighth floor.

Although the exact number of deaths is unknown, 146 bodies were found after the fire. Twenty-three of the dead were men, but the rest were girls from ages 13 to 23. Seven bodies remained unidentified.

Most of the young women at the Triangle Factory were immigrants of Jewish or Italian heritage. Many lived on New York's East Side, many blocks from the factory.

In 1911, laws requiring fire drills didn't exist in New York. Most workers at the Triangle Factory had never practiced how to escape the building during a fire. Today, businesses need to have fire alarms and an emergency action plan. The plan must include safe exit routes for employees.

The Asch Building, which housed the Triangle Shirtwaist Factory, was nearly fireproof. The outside of the building suffered only minor damage, though everything inside the structure burned. Today, the building is a National Historic Landmark and part of the New York University campus.

The fire of 1911 was not the Triangle Factory's first fire. Before March 25, Blanck and Harris reported several smaller fires at the factory. Building inspectors warned the men many times that their building was unsafe.

After the Triangle fire, the New York State Factory Investigating Commission was created. Commission members spent three years investigating factories in the area. They made 60 suggestions to improve workplace safety. Most of their recommendations were quickly adopted, including the addition of automatic sprinklers in buildings more than seven stories tall and doubling the number of fire inspectors. They also suggested new rules for lighting, ventilation, washrooms, and dangerous equipment.

Several unions worked together after the fire to form the Joint Relief Committee. This group gave money and aid to families and victims of the Triangle Shirtwaist Factory fire.

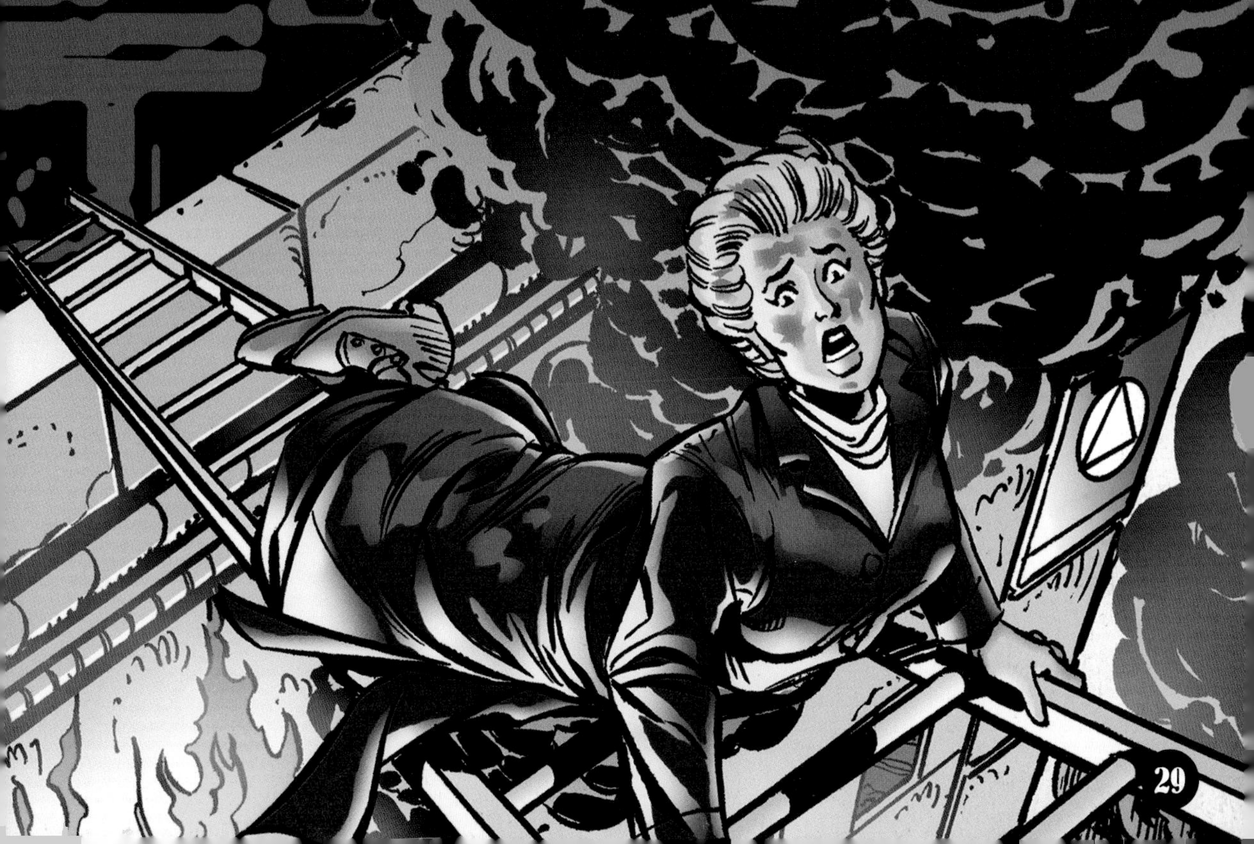

GLOSSARY

acquit (uh-KWIT)—to find someone not guilty of a crime

manslaughter (MAN-slaw-tur)—the crime of killing someone without intending to do so

mourner (MOR-nuhr)—a person who is very sad and grieving for someone who has died

strike (STRIKE)—refusing to work because of an argument or disagreement with an employer over wages or conditions of the workplace

union (YOON-yuhn)—an organized group of workers set up to help improve such things as working conditions, wages, and health benefits

INTERNET SITES

FactHound offers a safe, fun way to find Internet sites related to this book. All of the sites on FactHound have been researched by our staff.

Here's how:

1. Visit www.facthound.com
2. Type in this special code **0736854835** for age-appropriate sites. Or enter a search word related to this book for a more general search.
3. Click on the **Fetch It** button.

FactHound will fetch the best sites for you!